WOMAN 2 WOMAN

WOMAN 2 WOMAN

A conversation between friends

ELDER TEREASA BROWN

Library of Congress Control Number: 2015907340
ISBN: Hardcover   978-1-5035-6914-0
               Softcover   978-1-5035-6916-4
               eBook   978-1-5035-6915-7

To order additional copies of this book, contact:
Xlibris
1-888-795-4274
www.Xlibris.com
Orders@Xlibris.com
711610

This book is dedicated to my children and grandson: Alexus, Diamond, Calvin, Tatyana, and Jeremiah. Without them, life would be dull and unadventurous. They keep me grounded and focused on what it is I am supposed to be doing. I thank God for giving me such precious gifts, even when things are not always right in our home.

Contents

8. W2W Blogs

Acknowledgments

I also want to thank my mother, Geraldine, for always supporting me. A special thanks to my aunt, Phyllis, for listening to all these poems every night I came home from work.

Relationships

I Can't Take Care of You

I can't take care of you
Before God gave Adam a wife
He gave him a job
"Adam, name these animals"

Before man sits down to eat
he goes out and works a full day

You see, it would be wrong for me
to aid and abet you in being lazy

It would be wrong for me
to feed you and let you be fat and full
with no job

It would be wrong for me
To let you stay in my house and watch TV
while I go to work

It definitely would be wrong
for me to let you drive my car

You see, a man that doesn't work
doesn't eat
A man with no money
gets no honey.

A man with no car
means we're walking
And how can two walk together unless they agree

Bottom line,
I can't take care of you.

Forever

Is forever too much to ask?
How long will it take for you to know?
That forever is all I need.

Do you see yourself with forever?
Or are you still playing around with maybe?

Why toil with maybe
when forever can give you security.

Maybe brings doubts
Forever brings hopes

Toil with maybe too long
And never is all that you'll have.

Don't Let It Be Said Too Late

Don't let the words I love you
Be said too late

Don't let the words I'm sorry
Be said too late

Don't let the seasons change
And another one sees that,
I am the one they've been looking for
To complete them

Before it's too late, come for me
Before it's too late, apologize to me
Before it's too late, tell me I'm your everything

Wait!
It's too late, somebody beat you to it.

Liabilities

Oh no, you don't! Go treating me like a liability
I don't detract anything from you.

Don't you know?
Other men look at me as an asset
I add value to them.

If you want liabilities then go find them
I know how to add continuous value all by myself.

Sweetheart, I don't come at a discounted price
And I never go on sale.

I'm the real deal
My price is high
I'm good quality
My value never depreciates
And yet you say,
I'm a liability.

ELDER TEREASA BROWN

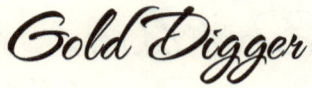

Gold Digger

He thought I wanted him for his money,
He didn't know I was sitting on Fort Knox

He thought I wanted him for his car,
He didn't know I like to run and walk

He thought I was a gold digger . . .

So, I wined him and dined him
I showed him the finer things in life

Now he's the one with the shovel

You Don't Want Me but You Need Me

Wasn't it you that said goodbye?
Wasn't it you that said you didn't want me?
But now you're in my office and you need me.

You try to have small talk and I stop you and say
Mister, how can I help you?

You see I mean business, so you get to the point
Again, here you go with the small talk

I quickly thank you for coming to my office
As I walk you to the door

I tell you in a sweet, soft, sexy voice
If you need anything else, please see my secretary on the way out
And remember, you don't want me but you need me.

I Was

I was a person before you ever came into my life

I was handling my own business
Before you ever tried to give me advice

I was making my own decisions about my life
Before you came at me with some shallow dreams

I was independent
Never dependent on a man
Now with my hand in yours
Here I stand

You showed me patience, love, security, and protection
You trusted in the Lord
To lead you in the right direction

You changed
I *was* to *we are.*

Revenge

You didn't know what to expect
When I said wait a minute,
wait a while

You thought, I would key your car
You know, I'm above that

You thought I would I fight the other woman
She didn't do anything to me
I have no problem with her

As you wondered
I sprang into action

I dropped forty pounds,
Wrote another book
Changed my look

And you say to me
You have a look in your eye
That I can be replaced

I quickly tell you
It's not a look,
You have been replaced

You've been replaced by success and freedom
Power and prowess

Something you can't compete with
Something that has me for good

So for now on, when you look at me
You're looking at revenge.

Thank You

Thank you for leaving me when you did
Now I don't have to share my success

Thank you for leaving me when you did
Now I don't have to get caught up in your mess

Thank you for showing out before we said I do
Now I don't have to play the fool

Thank you for pulling the curtains back on your act
Now I'm very happy by myself, and that's a fact.

This Is Not the Time

This not the time for you to come back around
After you've been gone so long

This is not the time for you to say you want this to work
Now that I have moved on and am happy

This is not the time for you to try and call my family
To get back in good graces

When you left, you said you were done
But I guess you realized you had it better at home
And now you want back in

Sorry, there's a new man's name on the lease
Maybe you know him, maybe you don't
At any rate, what you didn't want, he did
And just to make sure he kept it, he gave me his last name.

Expiration Date

When we entered into this relationship
We knew it wouldn't last forever

We didn't know if this would turn into love or marriage
But we knew it wouldn't last forever

We had good times, and we had bad times in this relationship
Yet, we knew it wouldn't last forever

When times were good, we were sitting on top of the world
We knew it wouldn't last forever

When times were bad, our relationship was on life support
We knew it wouldn't last forever

Now the relationship has come to an end
The expiration date has finally come
And all we can say is,
It's been real, and it's been fun
We knew it wouldn't last forever

I See but Don't Say

Because I see something
Doesn't mean I have to say something

I know how to sit back and observe
While making you think
You're getting away with something

You've given me a chance
To stack my evidence against you

So when I come to you
And say it's over
And you say please let's talk about it

I'll just tell you
Because I saw what I saw
I don't need to say
What the evidence has said

At What Cost

At what cost do I keep my mouth shut and act like I'm blind
At what cost do I keep letting you think
I don't know what you're doing
At what cost do I keep you in my life

I'd rather go bankrupt than live a lie
I'd rather lose it all than continue to sit here and cry
I'd rather be by myself than be showered by gifts, money, and lies

At what cost I ask myself
The price costs too much, and you're not worth it

Self-confidence

Outspoken

Some say she's loud
Others say she's aggressive
But ask her and she'll say
I'm just confident.

People will try to put you in a box
if you're not careful.
So she speaks her mind.

She walks with confidence
She holds her own in a crowd of people
Her presence commands the room
She's fierce, and she knows it
She doesn't break down because someone opposes her

Who is she?
She is outspoken

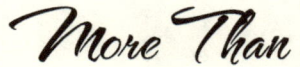

More Than

Am I not more than a text or app?
Am I not more than another notch on your belt?
Am I not more than an around the way girl?

Hold up! I just looked in the mirror
and the mirror said

I am more than worth the wait
I am more than big hips and big lips
I am more beautiful than all the rest

And, I am more than happy without you

What If

I've been hearing *what if* all my life
to the point that *what if* has become
a part of me.

I want a new me but *what if* won't let me go
I've tried to separate myself from *what if*
but I find myself staying in this crazy relationship

Today, I'm finally breaking it off with *what if*
And I'm starting a new relationship with *when I*

When I has more possibilities than *what if,* and I believe
I can make this relationship work.

Cracks in the Mirror

He doesn't want you to see
the cracks in the mirror
so he sleeps around

As long as I'm the life of the party
No one will ever suspect he says

They won't suspect that;
I'm afraid!
I'm inadequate!
I'm lonely!

And all I want is to see the mirror whole . . .

With every failure comes another crack
With every fear comes another crack

Why isn't the mirror broken all the way?

Then he discovers,
He can recover from the failures
He can recover from the inadequacies
He doesn't have to be alone

All of a sudden, the cracks
are going away

His confidence and renewed thinking
is helping to seal up
the cracks in the mirror

ELDER TEREASA BROWN

I Don't Need a Man

Where is your man?
And why are you raising those kids by yourself?

Listen here!
I don't need a man to take care of me
I make my own money
I pay my own bills
And I'm happy being me

You're not happy
You're lonely
That's what society keeps telling me

Just wait a minute here
I said I don't need a man
that's different than wanting a man

I just refuse to settle
I deserve the best and
I won't settle for less than

As I told you before
I just don't need a man

I Mowed the Grass

The grass is greener on the other side
Because I mowed it

No, I'm not the prettiest of the bunch
But I keep myself together
I never let the people see me looking out of order
Whether, I'm running to the mail box or going to the store
I mowed the grass

Freshly manicured nails
A fierce cut wig
I mowed the grass

It's really not about how the grass looks from where you're standing
It's about how you mow it, when you own it

A Special Order

He was used to dealing with women that come a dime a dozen
so he thought he could step to her any kind of way

He said: You're playing hard to get,
and she replied: I am hard to get

As time went on, he found out
She couldn't be found in the regular inventory
He found she wasn't on the showroom floor
So, he kept asking himself, why can't I have her

Soon he discovered, she's a special order
He said within himself, I have to offer her more than she has
I have to add to her value
As he thought about it, he came to this conclusion:

I don't have anything to offer her
I will only subtract from her
This is a special order I can't place

I Thought

I thought I couldn't live without you
So I hung on tight despite how you treated me

I thought I couldn't breathe without you
So I always stayed in your space

I thought I couldn't amount to anything without you
So I clung to every word you said about me

I thought, I thought, I thought
This is crazy
My momma didn't raise me this way

So I decided
Not only will I live without you
I will thrive without you

Not only will I breathe without you
I will get rid of my oxygen tank

Not only will I be something without you
Everyone will know my name

My god! Look at what I thought

A Woman's Worth

A woman is more than
breast, booty, hips, and lips

She is brains and beauty
Bold and yet calm

She's not the woman on the video
That devalues herself for fifteen minutes of fame

She's not the woman that's so broken
That she'll do anything to keep a man

No! She's a woman
She respects herself and rather works her fingers to the bone
Before she sleeps with a man to get her rent, lights, and cable paid

This is a woman's worth

Self-reflection

When Sunday Comes

Most people look forward to Sunday
Family dinners, church, and sports on TV

When Sunday comes for me
It means a phone call or a text
About my daughter who's a million miles away.

Why does Sunday represent so much doom and gloom for me . . .

Lord, there's nothing I can do,
So I'll just pray and go on throughout my week
And know the phone will ring when Sunday comes

It Costs to Be Me

To be me
You have to be willing to be alone most of the time

To be me
You have to be willing to give much and gain little

To be me
You have to be willing to be misunderstood
And apologize frequently

To be me
You have to be willing to put yourself last

No matter the price
I'm willing to pay the cost to be me

Dig Deep

I've realized that all of my goals
haven't been reached so I must
dig deep, keep my head on straight,
and get busy

I've realized that I've been too busy
trying to please others so I must
dig deep and make up in my mind
it's all about me

I've realized that I care too much
about what others think of me so I must
dig deep and quit caring
and do me

I've realized digging deep
may make me unpopular
but it will make me happy

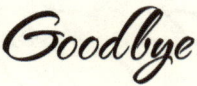Goodbye

Saying goodbye is sometimes hard to do
Saying goodbye is sometimes what we need to do
Saying goodbye doesn't mean the end of the world
Saying goodbye means saying hello to a brand new day, a brand new you

Say goodbye to say hello
To new opportunities
To new possibilities
To new love
To new life

Reality

Dealing with Me

Hanging around the crowd
and having lots of fun
I don't have to deal with me

Always on the go
No time to stop and think
I don't have to deal with me

Making sure I'm never alone
always have someone on the phone,
in the car, in my office
I don't have to deal with me

TV on, music going, kids playing
I don't have to deal with me

It's nighttime, I'm so tired
I fall asleep as soon as my head hits the pillow
I don't have to deal with me

I've awaken an hour later
Nerves shattered, now
I'm forced to deal with me

Truth Is

Truth is
You really don't want the answers to
The questions you keep asking me

Truth is
I'm going to start acting like what you call me

Truth is
Either I'm going to love you or respect you
But I won't do both

Truth is
This is not working and
I'm going to have to let this go

Truth is
When I really think about us
There really never was an us
We were just pieces to a puzzle
That never fit

I'm Not Impressed

You have a nice car with rims
That cost more than the car
I'm not impressed

You go to work every day
I'm not impressed

You take care of your kids
I'm not impressed

You say you know God
I'm not impressed

You display the characteristics of God
You talk openly about your relationship with God
You're not afraid to praise him in public
I'm not impressed

I'm in awe, dazzled and fascinated

Stranger

We don't talk by day
But you want to creep by night

You don't respond to text by day
But you knock on my door at night

You see me in passing
And act as if you don't know my name

Finally, we meet up
But I'm silent
You go to touch me
And I pull away

You say what's wrong
And I say

Momma told me never to talk to strangers
And I yell to the top of my lungs
Stranger! Danger!

Four Things You Can't Recover

1. The stone once it's thrown

2. The occasion after it's missed

3. The word after it's said

4. The time after it's gone

Everybody Said

Everybody told him what he couldn't do
But no one told him what he could do

Everybody told him what he shouldn't try
But no one told him what he should try

Everybody said they didn't count on him making it
But when he made it, everybody had their hand out

When he lost it all,
Everybody said I knew he was nothing

When he went to everybody he'd helped
Everybody said we don't know each other like that

It's All Good

So you walked out and thought I wouldn't amount to anything
You banked on me not being able to make it on my own

To your surprise,
I have more than I had when I was with you
You shutter at the fact
I haven't called you for anything

You hate the fact, that for me
Life is good
Being single is good
Having peace of mind is good

To sum it all up
It's all good

Teaching

Submit

Ladies, we treat the word "submit" as a dirty word
We say ain't no man going to tell me what to do
We say I ain't following no man

Well, when you "submit" to your husband
You're saying I submit to the mission that God has him on

Ladies, do you know your husband's mission?
Or are you hindering his mission?

So now, will you "submit?"

A Mother's Love

A mother's love is similar to Jesus' love.
She will go through hell to save her children.
She will love them unconditionally.
Sometimes when her children want to do things their way, she'll never say a word.

A mother's love will accept her children back with arms wide open, even after they've walked out rudely.
She won't say I told you so, but she will say let's pick up the pieces.

A mother's love won't help you do wrong, but will chastise you when you do wrong.
Her love will reward you when you do right.
She will make you feel like you are the only child she has, even if you have siblings.

A mother's love is what a child longs for and needs.

A Virtuous Woman

A virtuous woman is not
Coach, Dooney & Burke, or Michael Kors
She is like Louis Vuitton
She never goes on sale
She knows her value and her worth
So you will never see a price tag on her

She is universal wherever she goes
She can be spotted from a mile away

If you try to treat her like a knockoff
You might get knocked off

You can't go to your friends and ask about her
You can't go to your family and ask about her
You have to go straight to the manufacturer and get all of her specs
And then, you decide if you can afford her price

This is a virtuous woman

A Wise Woman

A wise woman doesn't spend hundreds of dollars on a purse
And can't afford to keep hundreds of dollars in it

A wise woman doesn't treat her kids like dirt
In order to be with a man

A wise woman doesn't use her tongue
To tear her kids or her man down to nothing

A wise woman shows her hands and arms
As a symbol of comfort
For a pat on the back or hug

A wise woman shows her feet and legs
As a symbol of endurance
No matter what, she keeps it moving along

A wise woman shows her heart
As a symbol of love
She continues to pour it out
After it's been broken over and over again

ELDER TEREASA BROWN

Through It All

Through it all
I carried the weight that no one else could carry

I held back the tears
I held back my fears

Through it all
I trusted no one
I confided in no one
I didn't believe in no one

Then one day
I met you in the midst of my sorrow
When I could no longer hold the tears back and you said

I've been here with you, through it all

Independent Woman

Society has told you
to be independent
So you got the education, the job, the house, and the car

Society told you
You don't need a man
And you listened to your girlfriends who could never keep a man

Oh! How independence have made you so happy and free
To do what you want
Go where you want
And live life on your terms

Now that independence has taken you as far as it can
Deep down inside you want a man
But you still keep listening to your girlfriends

You do know, with all of your education and money
Misery loves company

The Total Package

My friends say, girl, he's the total package
He has a good job, benefits, a house, car
and he takes care of his children

They really act like I'm desperate
and they're ready to push me off
on the first man they feel has the total package

After listening to them,
I respond boldly
All you've named were material things
He doesn't have character, integrity or morals
And most of all
He doesn't have a relationship with God

The total package!
Please! He only got pieces

Passion

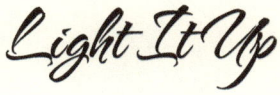

Light It Up

Don't turn off the lights
He whispered gently in my ear

I want to see your caramel skin
All undressed from your head
Down to your painted toes

Don't be ashamed of your body, he speaks softly
For if I wanted a picture
I would have painted one

But I want curves, the wrinkles, the dimples
And all that makes you, you

So, light it up
And let's turn out the night

Letters

A Love Letter to Me

Dear Self,

Look at you and look at what you've become. You are this strong, sexy, intelligent, and spiritual lady. I love the way you keep yourself up, and I love the way you stand firm when you believe you're right. You have a way to brighten up a room with your smile, and you always make people laugh. You spare no expense to make others happy, even when it means you have to put yourself on the backburner.

Whenever someone sees the cracks in your armor from all the trials you've had to endure, you never let them see the brokenness that makes you the brand new you. You are the type of woman that continues to look at the glass half-full. Always willing to lend a hand and lift others up when their down. I love being with you, we've had some good times and some bad times, but we've always managed to come out on top. I love the way you hold me and tell me that everything is going to be alright.

I love the way you cater to me as if I'm the only person in the world. I love the way you work hard all day, then come home and do some serious damage in the kitchen. You are such a beautiful woman from the inside out and head to toe. I just want you to know that I do take notice of all you do and I love you dearly.

Love Always,
Me

The Dog

Dear King,

Growing up, many young girls were taught that men are dogs. Therefore, as little girls we learned how to walk the dog, train the dog, and teach the dog. No one ever told us that men were princes. So when a prince came along, we didn't know how to treat him. We didn't know how to handle him treating us like a lady instead of an animal trainer. No one taught us how to take the prince and cultivate him and bring out the king in him. In so much, that the king was wasting away inside of him, because he was starting to conform to the dog that everyone said he was.

Ladies, it's time that we put our animal training skills away and bring out our cultivating skills. Princes are made to believe they will be king one day. They know they are next in line to rule. So instead of having a mindset of "no man is going to tell me what to do," we should have the mindset that the king has my best interest at heart, the king needs love, the king gets lonely, the king wants companionship, the king wants a confidante, and the king enjoys being intimate with his princess and only his princess.

When we began to value the prince in a man, the king starts popping out from time to time, and before you know it, the king will rule. Ladies, it is all right to let a man be a man. It's all right to let a man take the lead and make decisions. How will you ever know if your prince is ready to be a king if you always treat him like a peasant? I know this letter is a hard pill to swallow, but it's time out for keeping our men in the category of dogs, when clearly God has placed a warrior, protector, provider, and king inside of them.

Truth in Love,

Dear Children

Dear Children,

We have had the ride of our lives. We have traveled the world, and it wasn't without a price. I know you've had to lose friends and gain new friends. You've been the new kid in school numerous times, and yet you still managed to excel. I know you felt like I should have consulted with you every time we moved, but my job was to provide and protect you, nurture you and raise you in the admonition of the Lord. My job was not to get your permission on any decisions I made concerning our household. Oftentimes, you all thought I was the meanest thing on planet earth, and now you've come to realize I only meant it for your good.

I'm so grateful that God allowed you all to see the fruits of my labor; the staying up all night to finish a paper or get a project done. Sending you away all summer long so that I could go to school day and night, and not have to worry about not having enough time with you or neglecting you. You all were my inspiration to finish school. I refused to let life's circumstances hold us down and keep us living beneath our means. You often said, Mom, you're too hard on us. The truth of the matter is, I was being hard on myself and it just flowed to you all.

I pray that you see my failures and determine within yourself that you don't have to make the same mistakes I made because you've already lived them. I pray that you see my success and strive to be more successful than I can ever become. I pray that you see my disappointments and determine within yourself that disappointments may delay a thing but it certainly doesn't deny you of a thing. I pray you see my smile and know behind the smile stands a strong woman, a resilient woman, a protecting and caring woman, a woman who will go through hell and high water for you, and a woman that loves you unconditionally.

You are not the perfect kids but you are my kids, and I wouldn't have it any other way.

Love Always
Mother aka Madre, Padre

W2W Blogs

Are You FAT?

Do you consider yourself a FAT person?

Faithful - Can you do whatever God has called you to do no matter how small or large the task?

Available - Are you available and dependable even when it's not your turn to shine? Can you work behind the scenes and let someone else's light shine without saying what you did to make it happen?

Teachable - Are you too old to learn something new? Do you feel like I've been there, done that, I got a T-shirt to prove it? Do you look at the person who is trying to teach you something and say to yourself: You're kidding me, right? Go sit down somewhere, or who are you to tell me something you're not all that?

FAT people don't mind being *faithful*, *available*, or *teachable*. They understand that God could have chosen anyone to accomplish his mission but he chose them. They don't mind letting someone else get the glory because they know where their reward is coming from. They don't need their names in lights, because they realize they are servants and not celebrities. FAT people don't care who's doing the teaching as long as they are learning and can apply what they've learned to everyday living.

So I ask you again: Are you a FAT person? If not, it's not too late to gain some spiritual weight, and if you are, make sure to leave those spiritual diets alone; they only make you a SLIM person.

Shady
Lazy
Immature
Mediocre

Be blessed and continue to be a blessing.

The Spiritual Hospital

The church is the only hospital that has one doctor.

The doctor can see multiple patients at the same time and not violate any HIPAA laws.

He will have you go through a series of test and depending on how you do, you may have to repeat a few of them.

He will do some blood work, because the blood has power.

Don't worry about having insurance; the bill is paid in full.

The only thing the doctor asks of you is a "yes."

He always gives you the right prescription the first time.

The medicine may be hard to swallow at first, but continue to take it.

Some medicines take longer to work than others when you don't follow the instructions completely.

He has the cure you need.

He's the ultimate specialists, for he specializes in everything and every condition.

He won't waste your time telling you something that won't help you.

You won't need a second opinion.

If you take the doctor at his word, everything will work in your favor.

If you fail to take the doctor at his word, then the consequences could be dire; you could stay sick, bound or even die.

Some people may get to leave the hospital sooner than you, but don't worry you will be able to leave when it's your time.

Once your issue has been taken care of, you can always come back when another issue arises.

The doctor allows multiple visits, even if it's for the same problem.

His office hours are 24/7, 365 days a year.

Be blessed and continue to be a blessing.

It Doesn't Matter What You've Done

Stop letting people hold stuff over your head. If God doesn't hold it over your head, then you have nothing to worry about. There are so many lost souls that won't even step foot into the church because of hypocritical Christians who think they have a monopoly on salvation.

These Christians think they know the mind of God and act like they are his spokesperson and final authority on who can and cannot be blessed, saved, healed and delivered. The Bible says: Whosoever will let them come. That means: the whore, the liar, the pimp, the drug dealer, you, me, our kids, etc. God doesn't care what we've done. It's not his will that any of us perish. However, it may be the will of that sister or brother in the church jumping and shouting all over the place.

The Bible also says agree with your adversary quickly. So the next time those hypocritical Christians come telling you about yourself, say yeah, you're right. I lie, cheat, steal, etc. At least, I have the integrity to admit my sin. Unlike you, on the other hand, deceiving yourself thinking you are without sin.

Please don't let these people keep you out of the church or keep you from getting to God. Not everybody in the church is like this. There are some real people in the church that will tell you that we fall down and get back up. That some days you will give into temptation, that some days you will disappoint God and be disobedient, that some days you are going to want to walk away from the church and God, because of what you are going through and the pain seems too much to bear. And it's in those times that you have to cry out to God even more.

So, forget about what you've done and focus on what you're going to do for the kingdom of God.

Be blessed and continue to be a blessing.

Comfortable Airplane Ride

I fly a lot, and the single complaint I hear the most is the seats are not comfortable. These people paid for economy seats and expected first class leg room.

No one ever thinks about the pilot. He has an uncomfortable seat also. Have you ever sat in a cockpit? I have, I used to fix aircraft, and the pilots don't have first class seating either. Not only do they have uncomfortable seating, they have to multitask the whole flight to ensure we get to our destination safely.

Sometimes, we treat Jesus the same as we do the airlines. We want a comfortable ride. We give Jesus low economy praises, and we want him to give us first class blessings. We never ask him how he feels, and we don't realize he's constantly multitasking while getting us safely to our destiny. Whenever Jesus doesn't give us our first class blessing, we start complaining about how much we don't like the church and how many problems the church has.

Keep in mind, you can't come against God's church and think he's going to be OK with that. So stop looking for the comfortable airplane ride in the natural and the spiritual, if you are only willing to pay economy prices.

Be blessed and continue to be a blessing.

No

Do you have problems with telling people *no*? Are you afraid that people won't like you anymore if you tell them *no*? Do you help people out even when you don't want to?

No is one of the most powerful words in our vocabulary. It's all right to tell people *no*. People don't have a problem with telling you *no*. As a matter of fact, they will tell you *no* and expect for you to always say *yes*. The Bible teaches us to be meek not weak. God never called us to be door mats. People will try to use you because you are a Christian. For instance, if you tell them *no;* they will say, I thought you were a Christian. They try to play with your heart and emotions using that line, but don't fall for it.

If you have a hard time saying *no*, practice saying these:
No, I can't help you today.
No, I'm not going to let you keep using me.
No, I don't have to settle for you
No, I can't keep lending you money, I'm not the bank.
No, I can't cosign a loan for you; the Bible says that's foolishness.
No, you can't stay in my house, I don't run a hotel.
No, I refuse to take part in the auction lines at church described as offerings.

It may seem strange to say *no* at first, but keep practicing and it will become second nature.

Be blessed and continue to be a blessing.

Humble Yourself

When I was in the Army, my first sergeant would always tell me I need to eat humble pie. I disagreed with him because of pride, and I felt I was always right. Most of the times, I was right with what I said, but how I said it, was all wrong. I needed humble pie.

Life has a way to humble you. The Bible says to humble yourself under the mighty hand of God. Now, you can do this willingly or you can be forced. One way or another, you will be humbled.

God can use your health, your children getting in trouble, you losing your job and having to beg for help, your marriage, and the death of a love one or anything else he chooses to humble you. Don't let it boil down to that.

Tell God to lead you and guide you and to direct your path and speech. People may expect you to act up and flip out, but God expects you to drop your pride, show love and kindness, show meekness and act like his child.

Be blessed and continue to be a blessing.

Say What You Need to Say

Stop beating around the bush with people and stop sugarcoating what it is you need to say.

In today's society people want you to be real with them. The truth may hurt but it's out in the open.

Remember you are not Jesus so you don't have to speak in parables. Let your yea be yea and your nay be nay.

Be blessed and continue to be a blessing.

Defeat vs. Victory

Defeat says your enemies have prevailed. Victory says thou prepare a table before me in the presence of mine enemies.

Defeat says close your mouth and accepts the fact that you lost. Victory says shout with a voice of triumph.

Defeat says you've done too much wrong and God won't forgive you. Victory says I'm married to the backslider.

You have to make it up in your mind, that you've seen too many victories to let defeat have the last say.

Be blessed and continue to be a blessing.

Don't Throw It in My Face

Oftentimes, we do things for other people but then we have to make sure that they know it.

We may have helped them out of a bad situation, or with some food, or money, etc.

Next thing you know, we are holding them hostage with what we've done for them. We are quick to remind them that if we were not there when times were hard for them they wouldn't have made it. We tend to do this to our children, spouses, and let's not forget our fellow church members.

Have we ever stopped to think that God doesn't throw anything in our face but a mirror?

When he delivered us, did he ever throw in our faces that we were wretches undone?

When he healed our bodies, did he ever throw in our faces that he could have let us die?

When he died on the cross, did he ever throw in our faces that we were on our way to a burning hell? No! He said: Father forgive them for they know not what they do.

So on today, if you are going to do something for somebody, do it and then let it go. Don't throw it in their face because it could be you on the receiving end.

Be blessed and continue to be a blessing.

Your Name

Does your name mean anything? When people hear your name does it make them straighten up or do they say oh that's just her or that's just him?

Can people throw your name in the atmosphere and your name alone commands respect? Or is your name associated with being lowdown, scum of the earth, trickster, or shady?

Well there is power in the name of Jesus. Demons tremble at his name. People bow down at his name.

Did you know when you're in trouble if you call on the name of Jesus he will make a way out of no way?

I called him Jehovah Rapha when my heart was malfunctioning, and I found him to be a heart fixer.

Somebody else called him Jehovah Shalom when they were depressed and found he turned depression into peace.

Another person called him Jehovah Shammah when they felt all alone and they found out God was there.

Today, start calling on the name of Jesus from the smallest to the greatest of affairs that are going on in your life and see the power of God move.

Be blessed and continue to be a blessing.

Lord, Help Our Children

Today, I've spoken to so many different people, and everyone I spoke to had the same comments. Everyone was concerned about the state in which our children find themselves. Some of our children are dealing with domestic abuse situations, suicidal demons, sexual identity, gangs, drug addiction, alcohol addiction, promiscuity, diseases, etc., and the best weapon we got for this is prayer. We are the first line of defense for our children. So let us pray:

Lord, we come pleading the blood of Jesus over all of our children. Cover them and keep them. We cancel Satan's assignment over their lives. We come touching and agreeing that our children will not fall to the enemies' tricks and tactics. We decree and declare that our children will not succumb to drugs or alcohol. We decree and declare that our children will not commit suicide or homicide. We decree and declare that the gangs and the streets won't have our kids. We decree and declare that our children will finish school, they will know who they are and whose they are, they will be productive members of society, they will not be the neighborhood thug, and they will excel in all they do. Lord, help our children. Use them while their yet in their youth. Keep their minds, keep their bodies. Give us to be an example to them. Show them what true love is. When the enemy comes in like a flood, Lord, lift up a standard against the enemy. Lord, give us to never give up on our children and help us to raise them in the admonition of the Lord. In Jesus' name, amen.

We have to help each other to help our children.

Be blessed and continue to be a blessing.

Hard-to-Love People

Do you know someone that's hard to love? No matter how nice you try to be they always have something negative to say. Sometimes, you may find yourself going above and beyond to show that you love and care for this person. You prefer to love them from afar or just not deal with them.

Well have you ever thought that you were hard to love? That no matter what goes on you always have something negative to say. Have you noticed anyone going above and beyond to show you that they love you and care for you?

Well imagine this! At one point, we were hard to love but Jesus went above and beyond to show us that he loves us and cares for us.
No matter how negative we were, he said I love you.
No matter how much we complained, he said I know the plans I have for you.
No matter how much we resist him, he said behold I stand at the door and knock.
No matter how much we try to fight, he said why kick against the prick?
No matter how much sin we've committed, he said it's not my will that none should perish.

So before you decide to completely shut that person off because they are hard to love, think back when God could have cut you off but instead said I come that you might have life and that more abundantly.

Be blessed and continue to be a blessing

His Hands Are Bigger Than Mine

Stop trying to hold things in your hands, God's hands are much bigger and better. His hands have a way of making things all right no matter how detrimental the situation looks.

In my hands, my child is just nurtured, but in God's hands, my child is delivered.

In my hands, debt is paid monthly, but in God's hands, I'm debt-free.

In my hands, money just pays for things and is put into the offering tray at church, but in God's hands, it rebukes the devourer for my sake.

In my hands, the situation seems to be just enough, but in God's hands, the situation provides more than enough.

So take everything out of your hands today and place it in God's hands and watch him work miracles.

Be blessed and continue to be a blessing.

You Just Never Know

How many of us wake up in the morning and really know how our day is going to go? We may think we know or we may have some idea of how we would like it to go but we just never know.

You just never know when the phone rings what's going to be on the other end. You just never know if you will get off that phone call happy, mad, disappointed, confused, or in tears.

You just never know that when you started dating that person that they would turn out to be the best thing that ever happened to you or that you would have to run for your life.

You just never know that your boss has been watching you and decided to promote you ahead of your peers or fire you for taking paper, pens, and supplies home.

You just never know that while you are in fairly good health, all of a sudden your health fails without warning.

See, I just never knew so many good things and bad things would happen to me in life but at the end of the day, I would still have joy. I just never knew on February 27, 2012, I would undergo heart surgery at thirty-seven years old. I just never knew I would write out my own obituary just in case I didn't make it. I just never knew that I had to think about who was going to take care of my children and grandchild if I departed this world too soon.

The only thing I did know was that I gave my life to Jesus, and I didn't wait until I got sick to recognize I needed the Savior. So since we just never know, how about we choose to give God our life today because today could be the day that our soul is required of thee?

You just never know.
Be blessed and continue to be a blessing.

Other Books

On Your Best Day, You're Well Enough to Die

Don't Love Me to Death: When Teenage Dating Becomes Deadly

The Lord Is Speaking, But You Might Not Like What He's Saying